"Some stories fill the house of your body," writes Ellis Elliott in her breath-stealing new collection *Break in the Field*, and she should know. This gripping, heart wrenching exploration of her inner most thoughts and feelings while caring for her extreme needs stepson, "[whose] brain vessels shattered at birth into a million stars," are so raw, so deeply forthright, from a place of such compassion, tenderness, and introspection that I found myself tearful many times. "This is not about God's will or God / doesn't give you more than you can handle, / this is about cascades of drool and changing / a grown man's diaper." There is no self-pity on these pages, only a mother desperate to bring a shard of light and some semblance of beauty into an impossible darkness, while also dealing with the rest of life's challenges and sorrows. Still, ever the optimist, Elliott reminds us that even as we experience our worst moments "earth turns, peacock's show their plumes."

Kari Gunter-Seymour
Ohio Poet Laureate and author of
Alone in the House of My Heart

break in the field

Ellis Elliott

NOTES

The poem *Our Truest Hungers* is a combination of Found Poems, from the text of the book *The Boy in the Moon: A Father's Journey to Understand His Extraordinary Son* by Ian Brown, and atypical haiku in italics, intended as a type of "call and response."

In the poem *Cento for Julian*, lines are taken from the following poems: *Boy of Silence* by Barbara Mitchell, *Prosthesis Maker* by Willa Schneberg, *To the Curious People that Ask, "What do your Tremors Feel Like?"* by Eli Clare, and *For I Cannot Speak* by Aparna Upadhyaya Sanyal.

ISBN: 978-1-957224-12-1

Printed in the United States of America.

FIND US AT
oldscratchpress.com
devilspartypress.com

ACKNOWLEDGEMENTS

I am most grateful for the support of my family, especially my husband, Tim. My heartfelt thanks to my teachers and first readers: Cathy Smith Bowers, Ada Limón, and Morri Creech.

I am grateful to the editors and staff of the following journals in which versions of these poems first appeared:

Literary Mama: *Come Lay Your Hands*
Signal Mountain Review: *Or, Heard, Strike*
Spotlong Review: *Easy Fix, After Words, Our Truest Hungers*
Brushfire Literary Journal: *Almost Did*
Isele Magazine: *I Don't Know, Can You? God Comes to You*
The Ear Literary Journal: *On the Eve of My Son's Early-Onset Schizophrenia Exam*
The Ignatian Literary Magazine: *Hemorrhage*
Cider Press Review: *Dream Pilot*
The Rail: *Sweetgrass, Morse Code, My Mother Exhales*
Plainsongs Poetry Magazine: *Instructions on How to Be a Stepmom to a Disabled Son*
Streetlight Magazine: *Husk*
Perceptions Literary Magazine: *Cento for Julian*
Delmarva Review: *Back to School*
Euphony Journal: *Music Lessons*
Sierra Nevada Review: *Jehovah Slim, New Melleray*
I-70 Review: *Teaching Ballet to Children on Zoom during a Pandemic*
Apricity Magazine: *Sleepover*
Platform Review: *Holy Being*
Nude Bruce Review: *Turquoise Sweater*

CONTENTS

ONE

TWO

CONTENTS

THREE

An encounter with disability inaugurates a break
in the observer's perceptual field-
a tear in our being that reveals
the (body's) open-endedness,
it's incompleteness,
it's precariousness.

> -*A History of Disability*
> Henry Jacques-Stiker

Only what is human can truly be foreign.
The rest is mixed vegetation, subversive moles, and wind.

> *Psalm*
> Wislawa Szymborska

For Julian, and for all the caregivers.

In memory of my parents,
Willard and Lu Gatewood.

ONE

Hemorrhage

How the word looks
like bumper cars
of crashing consonants.
Like sandpaper on the ears
of your skin. Like a John Cage
song made from dead fish
on piano strings, rubber ducks,
and ice in a blender.
Like bad tap water in a foreign
country. Like carbonated
bubbles up your nose. Like teeth
on teeth. Like a surprise party
gone wrong.

Cento for Julian

In the beginning there was my son.

> I am not dead. I guess I'm lucky.

He grew to a pale shadow.

> I have a lot of time to think. Because there are many of us limbless ones.

I waited for his song, but his voice was a trapped bird in the throat.

> I cannot speak, but my body is a mudra.

Perhaps the world was too noisy for him.

> Hear me now, in the chants of a thousand monks praying for peace.

He never came out of his silence.

> Hear me now, in dry henna leaves breaking underfoot.

Tell me have you ever watched hands grow wild and loose?

> Explain to me your hands. I cannot imagine.

In the end there is only my son and all my grief sharpened to love

> For my body is a supple mudra that speaks.

Instructions on How to Be a Stepmom to a Disabled Son

Take one 8-ounce can vanilla PediaSure, viscous brown, and smelling of old milk and dryer sheets. Mix with microwaved Quaker oatmeal, cooled by two ice cubes. Stir.

> Lift open the kitchen window, let the pine tree's green breeze ferry the aroma.

Fill the barrel-like cylinder of the syringe, and take your time, pulling slowly. Watch the thick liquid rise. Tie the Carolina blue terry cloth bib behind his neck.

> Check the roman numerals on the circle of wall clock, estimate when to push his wheelchair outside for the bus.

Attach the greying feeding tube to the valve above his belly button that looks like those on bright pink inflatable swim toys.

Fill the syringe. Empty. Fill. Empty. Finish. Pull the tube. Close the valve.

> Close the window, place Grand Meme's quilt around his shoulders.

Stroke his stubbled jaw. Test the electric razor on the back of your hand. Hold his head in one hand to keep him still, use the other to shave.

> Kneel in front of him. Cup his curved, bare foot to pull up his purple Vikings sock. Wrestle on a black Converse high-top, and lace up.

Push him out the kitchen side door as the bus lift makes its slow slide to the ground.

Dream Pilot

Sometimes when I go to get him
he's asleep, among the papered walls
of azure and emerald hot air balloons.
His wild engines still silent, peace unseen
during waking, when arms seize
and legs contract. I hesitate to wake him
from his reverie of sleep or intrude
in his treasured inner rooms.
But sometimes he is sitting, his hand
tapping steady beats on the wall,
and when I flip the light switch he turns
to look at me, his hazel gaze locking mine
and I could swear that he knows me,
that he pilots every balloon ride toward home.

Julian at Rest

Sleep unfastens him
from the stiff knot of day,
and his jerks and tremors
slacken. His clenching
contractions slither off,
their work done.

In darkness, he sheds
the dissonant world.
His tangled electrical
signals loosen and float
like ribbons, as relief unrolls
its velvet bed of stillness.

Julian Dreams

In your dreams you float,
                     buoyed and secure
following the finless dolphin to the water cavern
                    limbs loose and tremorless.
You spin forward and down,
                              an undulating merman.

Water the color of peacock courses cold
                  into your ears to soothe
                      the fiery brain, release
contracted muscles. Ligaments lengthen,
                  sinews thaw, supple
                    and joyous.

As you swim to the surface:
                  a flood of words.
They jump and arc like fish onto the boat,
                    filling the bow.

Sweetgrass

She bent silvery green sweetgrass leaves
into woven baskets in a ritual as rote

as a low-country Sunday School hymn.
Both held and pulled with her right hand,

the coils must be taut with tension and strong
enough to hold water. She sketched rooms

to scale in her red spiral notebook, sewed
the teal silk curtains, and died in the house

I moved into. In the kitchen were her copper
cooking pots, her cracked oyster plates,

her mint green matchbox from Paris,
her baskets on cabinet tops, and her three

lost boys. I search for something sturdy
to contain their grief. And when it can't be found,

I become my own flawed variation. My broad
leaves braid and curl around all of us.

Easy Fix

This is what I'm looking for, the SuperBrainOmeter
to produce a ticker-tape explanation of him.
Use soothing words, please, like lullaby and sugared
violets. Not like hemorrhage and thalamus bleed.
Although they have a slight allure.

He has no smile or grimace to illuminate my way,
only clear, hazel eyes. One fixed, one following.
May I have your attention for a minute? I ask
the fixed eye, *I have a few questions.* The answer
is clear burnished copper, with a jade green sheen.

Static

In science fiction movies about aliens,
                    the experts look for patterns
in the zigzag of high and low sound
                    frequencies on computer screens.

Julian cannot talk,
but his father says his noises are like this.   Loud
staccato bursts at first,
then

slow sustained notes, as he turns his head
        to his inner tempo.

In movies, sounds from aliens call to us
        through static clicks and trills meant to be mysterious
codes destined for translation. A murmur,

        like the half-heard conversation at the table next to yours,
        or the unknown messages sent through roots between trees.

There is always the desire to glean
        meaning or find something more.

From pulsed whale calls,
        dolphin chatter,
        and birdsong we cobble understanding.
What we perceive as *stay away*
        or *come near* comes down to
        I am here.

Julian's Possible Superpower #3

Making time stand still works well with rain.
Expecting the drop's demise, instead surprised

when they choose to suspend midair
just shimmering there like sequins

on his cousin's recital costume. Dance
works well for slow motion, limber

legs bend in plié, push off to launch
and ascend. Here he revs up revolutions,

she spins faster, higher now toward
bright stage lights. While he sits below

showered in sweat and loose glitter,
her motion becomes his and, lifted

by applause, he floats beyond the wheel
chair. Once again, he stops time.

Relative

I ordered one of those 23AndMe DNA kits and found out I'm
directly related to Jesus.
                              -husband, Tim

Maybe not
directly,
although,
in the sharp
heat of a North
Carolina summer
afternoon on
the porch, when
you knelt to peel
the thin cotton socks off his pale, slender
feet, lifting from the footrest
of his wheelchair, and cradled in the palm
                    of your hand,
                        your lips blowing
                          a cool stream of air
                        onto first one,
                      then the other, I knew
                    you were at least somewhere
on that particular DNA chain.

Navigation

My son is absent
words, instead:
          burst of snorts
          guttural groans
          feathered trills
          bass-note grunts,
cacophonous and
constant.

He is the polished prism
of a circling lighthouse lamp.
His repeating, rhythmic sounds
flash signals to steer my swaying
mothership back to him.
I keep
returning
until my boat
begins breaking apart.
I keep
returning
until it splits open plank
by plank with a ripping shriek,
until all I hear
is ringing.

TWO

Strike

Some stories fill the house of your body
like smoke, the smell of cigarette rising

up the carpeted stairs from the kitchen,
ice crackling from plastic tray to glass.

Regular as ballet class and homework, I waited
in my room for her steps up to bed, my shallow

breath background sound for dread. In the flicker
of half sleep I was sure her heavy lids, unsteady

fingers would go slack, the lit tip fall, again.
This time sure it would not stop at scorched

carpet or sheets with buttonhole burns, sure
I would feel the blurred heat first.

Some stories live in your bones like fire
on a North Carolina winter night. My father's

tale of the thunderstorm that hit the farm
after Christmas. How he played with his

toy train on the oval terrain of the brown
and gold braided rug by the hearth. How lightning

struck and sparks circled the track, surrounding
him before disappearing. How he froze, unable

to speak, how seventy years later he could feel
the hot current run under the thin flesh of his hand.

Some stories slide thick from behind to settle like black
tar down my fully-grown spine, how they no longer ignite

with bending or excess heat, but stagnant
and unwilling to go, resigned to the staying.

Or

I was afraid the house
would burn down
or that it wouldn't.
Fear that smelled
of Jim Beam
and Kent Regulars
and felt like fists
of stinging nettles
in my twisting child
size gut. Never thinking
past her hot ashes
falling from cigarette
to mattress. Then,
it could be over, the flare
gun of my flaming
house would tell
the story I could not.

Heard

Trish and I could almost stand upright
in the wide, concrete cylinder
of the drainage pipe running under
our steep street. We loved to sit inside
on the curved edge and experiment
making sounds, mouths open wide
to howl or lips pursed to whistle.
We yelled *I love Benji Hanson* or sang
the chorus to *Dancing Queen*. Syllables
circled our private grotto, pierced
the cool fall air, and seemed to fill
galaxies.

We loved best when football fans
would walk down our street coming
home from the game, and we'd wait
beneath, suppressing giggles until
they passed over the grate above us.
Together, we threw our lawless chorus
upward.

Later, deciding whether to wear
painter's pants or overalls to school
the next day, we remembered what
it felt like to have a voice so powerful
it made knees buckle. We remembered
what it felt like to be heard.

I Don't Know, Can You?

Mrs. Lewis would say whenever we asked
Can I use the restroom? in 7th grade math,
forcing us to say *may we,* which we reenacted
repeatedly, but never forgot. Aaron sat between
Trish and I on the row closest to the door, with
his shiny brown hair slicked back and wearing
polyester plaid high water pants. His job
was go-between for passing carefully folded
notes, his low arm swing casual, but calculated.
He took his job seriously, as we did ours.
Many times, while Mrs. Lewis stood at the board,
he would begin an almost inaudible humming
of *Swing Low, Sweet Chariot.* Sometimes,
amid the din of passing Tyson Chicken trucks,
she would turn. She would ask if someone said
something, and we knew she had heard him.
We always shook our heads *No* and shrugged.
Our unspoken agreement held fast, balancing
our young selves on the edges of how we can
learn the rules, how we may break them, and
how we could and might be heard.

Thriller Thursday

in junior high meant Mark Meineke would put
his arm too tight around me in the cold dark
of the Malco Theater on College Street. He already
sported beard stubble, and a swagger born of
parents never home. It was thrilling to imagine
his house, with a permanently parked lawnmower
in the yard, his mom asleep with a half-lit cigarette
in her mouth, and SpaghettiOs congealed,
half-eaten on the stove. His untethered life felt
both foreign and seductive, his whispered drawl
said *"c'mon,"* as his lips glazed my ear. Like the knife
glistening right outside the bedside window,
there was a feeling this story could go either way.
And all along, the flickering movie screen spelled
it out in front of me. Watch for warning signs. Turn
on lights. Do not stumble as you run away.

Sleepover

Mr. Morchek, already stooped
from arthritis, curled over
the pot on the stove, steam
on his glasses, and stirred opaque
soup for our sleepover dinner.
We sat waiting, comparing nail polish,
while my friend's older sister set
the table. No one mentioned their
mother, who had left months ago
and gone home to Mexico. No one
spoke of it, but both sisters wore white
linen shirts she had made, with
explosions of dainty embroidered
coral flowers and apple green leaves.
And then, like bright colors on skulls
for a Day of the Dead celebration
of what was once there, but now
is gone, he took his chair at the head
of the table, while hers, at the other
end, sat empty.

Jehovah Slim

Perhaps you've forgotten his name, but you remember
the crunch of his mile-long olive Chrysler in your gravel
driveway every Sunday after lunch. You knew he looked
like Slim Whitman, a has-been singer you'd seen on TV,
stretched tall with slicked back, coal-black hair. You knew
he always wore a thin white button-down shirt with a bolo tie,
usually with a turquoise stone, but sometimes onyx with tiny
painted horses. When he came to your front door the first time,
he held *The Watchtower* pamphlet up for your father to see
as he explained the urgency of salvation. Your father cut him
off mid-sentence, as you wound around to peek from behind
his legs. *I respect your beliefs, but they're not mine. How much?*
Slim kept on coming for years. Your father would have the dime
ready, ask about his family and he'd ask about yours. If he missed
a Sunday, your father would ask if all was well when he returned.
Slim kept coming, knowing there was no conversion here, and
your father kept answering the door. Now, years later, if you avert
your eyes at the man splayed out on the park bench, find yourself
fuming because the repairman is late, or you whisper to complain
in the Wal-Mart line about *those kind,* you might remember to do
as your father did. Take the pamphlet. Ask about their day. Listen.

After Words

1. Kathleen at the hair salon knows when she swishes the blue-black styling cape around me to always move to the first snap, so the thin hem of collar does not touch my neck.
2. The larynx looks like a fortune cookie poised on top of the trachea in the neck. Hollow, it is commonly called the Voice Box.
3. My middle son insisted on wearing his Woody the Cowboy pajamas to Miss Penny's Preschool every day for a week. My oldest son wore a black cape with red satin lining that his grandmother made. He wore it for years. He said it made him feel powerful.
4. Afterwards, at work, my half-words hung suspended and unformed from my lips. My coworker Dorothy fretted, circling her palm on my back, and offering cold water.
5. Air travels from the lungs up into the trachea, and then through the larynx. Muscles contract in the larynx to manipulate vocal cords into making sound.
6. I remember the light from the pole in the parking lot of my first apartment in midtown Memphis fracturing in flashes and reflecting off a nearby window. I remember his hands fit easily around my neck. I remember my vision blurring like a rain-streaked windshield. I remember my back on the wet asphalt and the raspy huff I made as air returned to my windpipe.
7. If you place your middle finger just past the center of the front of your neck and press, it will become uncomfortable and you will cough. If you place the thumb behind the neck and press with four fingers in front, the sensation intensifies.
8. The first time, Kathleen placed the styling cape collar on the third snap. My breath quickened and I used my index and third finger to quickly pull it off.
9. When I told my sons about what happened twenty-five years later, I still used the word "mugging" instead of "assault." The police told me to just be glad all they wanted was my car.

When Your Mother Buys You Self-Help Books Instead of Talking

Smart Women, Foolish Choices simply means
I want you to think again about your choice of college
boyfriend. I know he's your first love, but he won't
be your last. I hope you know all the fire of new love
is fun, but always comes to an end. Bet on it.
Act Like a Lady, Think Like a Man simply means
now that you're divorced, think twice about yoga
pants. You've had three children. And, lower your
laugh. Steve Harvey says it's okay to be independent,
just not too independent. Look into it, and for God's sake
quit smoking. You look like a dragon. Love is like that,
consuming in blazing breaths, like my love for you. I fly
circles overhead, not knowing any other way than this,
scorching fields below with messages in smoke.

New Melleray

Their voices lifted and ricocheted off the cold
stone walls of the abbey as Trappist monks sang
at services seven times a day. They lined each side
like perfect white teeth, and the slant of sun struck

arches of leaded glass to bounce back in swirls off
the black granite altar. Outside my sparse room
of metal bed and beveled windowpanes, diligent
snow-covered cornfields stood guard. I had come

seeking order, a certain solace found in ritual,
and devotion dressed in crisp robes. My own life
was a simmering litany of unsatisfied appetites,
always too much and never enough. I craved

belief like theirs, strong enough to rise at three a.m.
and to sing. Guests were invited, so I shook sleep
and sin off like a bear wresting itself from hibernation,
and joined them. My animal self was not gone,

but restless, and ravenous. I sent my voice high
like a long dormant hymn, more growl than song.

On the Eve of my Son's Early-Onset Schizophrenia Exam

The plumage of my devotion unfurls
inside a canopy of tangled tree branches.
My ragged wings reach to hide the moss-
covered nest of my son's shiny eccentricities.
My delicate spine curls to cover his disparate
offerings; scraps of tinfoil, gold nib of fountain pen,
and the shifting hues of a hummingbird feather.
He hears them, insistent shards of sound coming
closer, voices circling and lifting from roots below.
The funnel clouds of chatter rise. With your small
body tucked beneath mine, I take off, while I still
think we can outrun this, while my talons clutch
your soft belly so tight they draw blood.

Blanket Fort
Pandemic Poem, 2020

My son calls from his glassy high-rise
on FaceTime to show me the blanket fort
he and his girlfriend built the night before.
Outside, the doors of the world had shut,
orange tape crisscrossed playgrounds,
and balconies spilled with singing. Inside
apartment five was a fraying blue sheet
for sky spread over couch cushions and
Amazon boxes. He told me they propped
pillows underneath to watch a movie online,
talked about what to order for dinner,
and where they were going to work out
now that the gym was closed. Outside,
the forest floor fills with long shadows
and a shard of moonbeam. Leaves crackle
underfoot and far off, the wail-screech
of a barn owl echoes like a siren. I have
taught him the way of the woods by star
shine. Now he must navigate on his own.
I tell him *be safe*, and hope he stays in
to sit by the flickering laptop light.

Teaching Ballet to Children on Zoom During a Pandemic

You wait while you watch
the ceiling fan of Namyla's
living room. From somewhere,
you hear a woman's voice trying
to get her daughter's spindled legs
into a pair of too-small pink tights,
finally found in the clothes hamper
beside a single ballet shoe. *She's ready,*
you hear, as Namyla's left side only
comes into the frame. You observe
the miniature portrait gallery
of limber loose limbs ready
to spring, as if they could catch
hold of a ceiling fan blade,
and fly away from four walls. I ask
all to press their hands to mine
on the screen at the same time.
Can you feel me? they ask.
Yes, I say,
but I don't.

Today, Let's Try This

You do not have to demonstrate
jumps, sure feet of perfect pencil
points. You do not need to worry
about the arabesque's exquisite line,
from peeling polished fingertips
to stretched toes. You do not need
any particular posture today, Victoria
and Namyla and Diamonique, Paris
and Rahkayla. No corrections, no body
shouldn'ts or shoulds. Instead, collapse.
Become shape-shifting poems risen.
Invite your weight, your newfound
breasts and hips, to sink. Write your
names on silted sand in octopus black ink.
Write your names across this new day.

Back to School

For the purple polka-dotted
welcome-back-to-school signs
festooned on doors.
For the teacher in Uvalde who
said she locked her classroom door,
how every night her dreams rehearse
her hand on the knob.
For bulletin boards filled with wide-
ruled stories of summer adventures.
For the desks in Uvalde, piled with
gold-stickered certificates from
awards day, and for the students folded
underneath. For the girls excited
to get Mrs. Grundy next year, because
she lets you make macrame plant hangers
and put your head down after lunch.
For the janitor in Uvalde, sobbing
in the supply room, as he watches
the water run red to clear from
the mop in his gray utility sink.

Mother Exhaled

and the smoke lifted into sunlight, slanting
in hazy prisms from the carved corners
of her Waterford crystal ashtray. To my young
self, it was an oracle's cauldron conjuring
messages in fire and clouds. Once, I sat beside
her upturned palm and read her lifelines, her skin
like rolling paper. Toward the end, she sat
alone in her ash-wounded recliner at night. She kept
her hand-carved cane close and by the glow
of the yellowed linen lampshade, she blew smoke
rings. She knew by then it was too late. She knew
the spell had already been cast.

.

Turquoise Sweater

She kept asking for the turquoise sweater
with square tortoiseshell buttons,
and I kept saying, *I'm looking*. As if
there were any place to look besides
the narrow, standard-issue wardrobe
in her bland nursing home room.
I chose not to tell her about her condo
floor filled with boxes and garbage
bags, or the friends backing up the truck
to load the freezer. I did not tell how my
brother and I had sorted through and boxed
her photograph albums, her yellowed
letters with grandmother's cursive,
or her jewelry. I did not tell her about
the twelve pairs of scissors we'd found,
or the bulging manila folder of her
nursing school papers. Not the ruby-red
Fostoria glassware in the kitchen cabinet,
not the ten boxes of instant-Jell-O in the pantry,
not the turquoise sweater with square
tortoiseshell buttons, and most of all, not
the multiple trips to *Goodwill*. I think she knew
it was gone. Both of us practiced in the truths
we were hiding, as if rehearsing lesser agonies
might ease the letting go.

Morse Code

It's been buried almost a year now under
the Kleenex box and pile of books on the table
beside my desk. It took a year for me to look inside
the red steno pad, the one missing its back cover
and always beside her at the nursing home.

It was filled with words written by others,
like her caregiver, nurse assistant, or me:

Her weight, month by month.
Medication List.
Book Recommendations for the Kindle, *Becoming, Hipbillies,*
Front Row at the Trump Show.
Six-line large, block print letter reminders:
PT-Fri. 10 a.m.
Razorback basketball game, 6 p.m., ESPN
Podcast Recommendations: *Hidden Brain, On Being.*

It was filled with words she wrote, her once smooth curl
of cursive, now sharp angles of stops and starts,
words she called me to remember,

What's the material my blanket is made of?
One page, one word: flannel

What is that nice man-nurse's name?
One page, one word: Trevor

Each page written in black Sharpie,
one bleeding into the next. A faint
imprint of the words that came
on the page before, then dots
like Morse Code, then page
after page, empty.

Husk

She was a day past presence, riding
the jagged breath below the surface
of consciousness. I was running
to make the next plane to Arkansas,
my frantic airport pace pulled by
a thousand thinning cords to home.
I was running, gunning the rental car
through the curves of the Ozarks,
clench-gut determined to make it,
for her to hear the familiar cadence
of my voice. She was inside her last
flickering, the holding place beneath
skin papered over bone. Her skull
was a half empty nest propped
on a pillow with the tempo of slowing
wing beats, until I ran through her door.
She gave a violent jerk at the sound
of my voice, and it was as if the words
themselves had shed their warm husks
and were reduced to pulsing threads
between us, from the hollow dark
where we first met.

Mockingbird

Ada reads in writing group about hiking
Sunset Ridge with her late son. She reads
about spiderwebs, views from the ridgeline,
and chestnut warblers with yellow crowns.

It is here, mid-sentence, her bird call bursts
forth, tongue curled to imitate its short
chip notes. Or spotted on topmost branch
of pine, with pursed lips, the whistled

flute song of hermit thrush. Her practiced
pitch becomes our shared hymn of grief.
I wish myself a mockingbird to her thrush,
to mimic hers, with my own long, drawn cry.

Nureyev at the Orpheum
Memphis, 1987

Two men sat in the row in front of me
near the aisle; one, in a sapphire cardigan
had his arm around the other, pulling him
close as they both sobbed. We were watching
Nureyev, who was nearing fifty then, and known
as one of the greatest ballet dancers of all time.
I was young, just out of college, and didn't
understand their tears. I thought it could be
because the famous Russian defector was past
his prime. His coil and spring less precise,
and the flagrant fling of his crimson cape
imperceptibly off tempo. Or, it might have been
the nearness of beauty, the push and pull of legend
etched in every articulated muscle. Now, as my body
begins its own slow defection, I sit between those two men.
I rest my head on the one free shoulder, as we all feel
the cape of our aging bodies begin to slip to the scratched
wooden stage floor, and into a puddle of what lies
between beauty and loss. It is a place so beautiful, I weep.

After the Hurricane, Hibiscus

blooms droop like shreds of popped balloon,
and the front door light hangs askew.
Inside, the marble floors of my body
have shifted, too. The incessant march
of warnings on TV don't bother me as much
anymore, and I settle in to watch it come
closer, to marvel as the rain gauge rises
and the bird bath overflows. It comes
whistling by on its way, elsewhere.
While I am here, hands pinching dead
blossoms and dragging my ladder
toward the broken light.

THREE

Come Lay Your Hands

"Jesus changes everything" Joyce Meyer, televangelist.
"except Julian's diaper" Tim, father of 17-year-old Julian, who
cannot walk, talk, or feed himself.

Oh, come lay your hands upon him,
speak in tongues and song
and ancient words,
  bring your creeds, your rituals, your holy smoke and
  incense
  raise him high, kneel down low, rock him in your arms,
bow at his feet,
  baptize him in water, anoint him in oil,
    lift him up, sit him in a sweat lodge,
      print his name on the list, circle up,
       and phone-tree him,
with prayer,
let that prayer grow loud and enormous,
  a monster to envelop everything in its path,
    place pins in him that correspond with systems both
    spiritual and physical,
join your words, your thoughts, your prayers into a groundswell of
unity,
  email this list to your seven best friends, don't
    walk under a ladder or look in a cracked mirror,
    but do
pick up a penny, pick the number seven,
read from your books, scriptures, and verses, chant and ring bells.
Give it your best shot.

Oh, harness your codified, swirled circles
  of energy that pop across eternity, cacophonous
  and unwieldy as Godzilla in downtown New York City.

Let them

       rain down in snowflakes upon his face,
       blanket him in paper confetti of prayers
       and tears turned whispers in his ear,

be sure no one is looking when you tell him the truth,
you are powerless and cannot change him.
He has changed you.

Prominent God

Julian has never laughed or cried. He has never talked and cannot communicate. His affect is flat and facial expression does not change. -Physician Statement, Power of Attorney

There is no right way to read
the Tarot. Eventually everyone
develops their own technique
You create your own stories
using symbols in the deck

> *I think he's glad to see you. That's a smile. Is that a smile?*
> (His full lips, one lifted edge)

The card projects perceptions

> *It's obvious he doesn't like Trump. I can just tell by what*
> *he does when he hears him on T.V.* (His head full of thick,
> wavy hair, turns. Eyes unfocused)

You need to bring
yourself into the cards

> *This is how we communicate, one pat for Yes, two for No.*
> *He does it only for me.*
> (His palm pats hers, smacking sound)

The cards give you structure
in which you can explore
your own questions

> *What if he knows everything that's going on?*
> *Suppose he knows a lot more than we think he*
> *does? What if he's a God?* (His dark hazel eyes, one
> fixed, one adrift. The fixed one lingers on yours)

Scan the cards and
absorb your reactions

> *He looks like he needs something.* (His
> vocalizations become louder, his muscular neck
> rocks violently side to side) *Is he hungry? Is he
> tired?*

The act of following a ritual
and treating your cards with
respect can change how you
perceive the world

> Lit by sliced sunlight, each morning his father strokes his
> slender fingers to wake him. (*The Sun Card: when we turn
> the light on in our mind we are enlightened. The Sun is a
> prominent God. You see and understand all that is
> happening within.*)

After you allow your
reading to process,
place the cards face down.

Anthem for the Man Who Said My Writing Might be Crossing the Line

This is not about God's will or God
doesn't give you more than you can handle,
this is about cascades of drool and changing
a grown man's diaper, this is not about crossing
your line, this is about when the line is mine alone
to cross. This is not about convincing you how much
I love my child. This is about truth when heads turn
away and eyes flinch, undone by the sight of him.

This is not about becoming educated in how to write
about my child, ways that will not offend, ways to speak
about my child who cannot speak for himself. This is about
every mother, everywhere, and the dreadful dark we find
ourselves in sometimes. This is not about keeping our stories
buried because of someone else's opinion on what
is appropriate to say out loud.

This is me saying it can be dreadful. This is me
saying it is often dark. This is me making him
real, giving him the only voice
he will ever have. This is me screaming for him
because he can't,
this is me,
screaming.

Almost Did

I am in the bathtub for the third time tonight. It's 3:00 a.m. and
what feels like a dense, spiked ball has wedged just below my ribs
and lodged firmly in place, undecided on how to escape. My   only
relief is below the steam of this rising water. My back presses to
the cool white curve beneath me, and I think of Marge and Joe
Porter, our neighbors in Athens when I was five, and their four
dirty kids: Joey, James, John, and Jenny, all under eight. The boys
liked to fight by the creek behind our house. They wore orange
Kool-Aid lips and always had something stuck in their hair. The
story goes that Marge fell asleep in the tub one night with her
ashtray and Whiskey Neat balanced on the ceramic rim, and I
imagine her lulled by her own quiet breath after the bedtime
struggle with the kids and her own despair. Now, she was finally
alone with her melting breasts and flaccid belly, maybe the scent of
lavender. Her eyes grew heavy, weighed down in surrender and
relief, and her chin dipped to her chest. She drifted under as the
water began to overflow until she gasped and sputtered awake.
Nothing happened to her, except it made for a good story the adults
liked to tell, and it followed me forty years later. Nothing
happened, but it almost did.

Burst

A million trillion times as bright
as the sun, cosmic gamma-ray bursts
are the most energetic and short-lived
in the universe. Your brain vessels
shattered at birth into a million stars,
just like that, a trillion ideas of you lost
in cosmic minutes. Hope flashes like
comets, or bonfires, or candlelight.
Maybe moonlight on sugared snow.
Let's pretend it is poetic, sublime. Pretend
in darkness we see a glint. Pretend you're
a universe we're not meant to know.

Our Truest Hungers

1.

the crisis of so-and-so's unhappiness
                                    pales
                                    next to my son.

(Boy
            recalibrates
                        world)

the opinions
matter less and less the more
you walk down the street
with a boy whose lumpy looks
attract attention.

*She waits by the phone
while her bathtub overflows,
the pink moon rises.*

you hold
your child's body,
hold its flesh and heat
close, like a skin
of fire, because
you need to hang on
to what life
there is.

the need to eat drives us,
sex makes us shameless,
but touch is our truest hunger.

Sitting beside her
deathbed, our fingers laced
the last true prayer

3.

I had to find a place for him
to live, outside our home.

seven years it took to get
to the most painful thing
I've ever done

The most painful thing
sits beside relief in the front
row, holding hands.

4.

he is an experiment
in human life
lived in the rare atmosphere
of the continuous present.

few survive.

Time, the magician
pulls bright scarf after bright scarf
from his black top hat.

5.

Minda,
my new god,
refused to refer
to any potential group home
he could move into
as just his house.
she says, *it'll be*
your house, too,
and I will find it
for you

> *Four ways to find God.*
> *Watch a spider spin her web.*
> *Taste rain. Ask. Grieve.*

6.

Minda said when she met us
it was as if the roof
was coming in.
Who admits
they've had a child
and can't raise him?

> *If this is our fate,*
> *put us down, but then earth turns,*
> *peacocks show their plumes.*

7.

I'm a wreck.
it is as if the shape
he gave my life, this deep fate
he handed me, is melting.

this house without him,
my body a cave.

> *My body a cave*
> *like a singing bowl, empty,*
> *notes of him, ringing*

8.

I can remember nights
                I was so far gone,
spent and totaled,
                I started to laugh.

A madman. Christ,

I was so tired:
                I remember lifting my legs
                to go up the stairs,
                as if they were hefty stumps.

I remember thinking:
I can't do much more of this.

> *Seen as madman, Christ*
> *was weary like the rest of us,*
> *did not float, but walked*

9.

The shaman lit a pipe and began
a long incantation.

I see a lot of elders.
They have come to see him.
This is the path
he has chosen for himself.

The interpreter asked
if I had questions. I said,
What about this new group home?
Is this good for him?

The shaman said,   *It will change his path,*
                     but his path is his path.
                     He has to go down his own path.

For the first time,
someone wasn't trying
to fix him.

Instead of trying
to make him better
or diagnose, it was what
and who he is.

It wasn't triumph
or tragedy.
It just was.

                         His path is his own
                         Trees point the way, speak languages
                         only he understands

.

10.

I knew
I loved him,
and I knew
he knew.

I held sweetness
in my arms,
and waited.

          I held sweetness once,
          I carry the beautiful
          inside me like winter

God Comes to You

disguised as your life, and dressed
in a heavy robe of red silk brocade
with pockets, inside and out, filled
with wine corks and old keys,
your son's baby teeth and your first
engagement ring, your Mom's damp
cocktail napkin, your Dad's 1972
McGovern pin, and a crumpled pack
of Marlboro Lights, until the day comes
you begin to empty every pocket piece
by piece. You hold each in your palm,
pausing before the clatter to the floor,
before stopping to slide the silk robe
off your shoulders only to realize
you are left as you've always been,
perfect and holy.

Music Lessons

I can tell you about the student learning
to conduct a symphony, told to practice
by holding a bag of beans in her palm
in order to feel the weight of the notes
in her body. It intrigues me to think
of the heft of crescendo, ascending
decibels gathering upwards, and whether
they float or seem tethered as she lifts
her arm before the inevitable descent,
whether it strikes at the center of her
sternum and drops like a silver pinball
to her belly. I can tell you the weight
of grief lodged between my ribs, changed
in time from puddle to solid, palpable
beneath the surface of my skin. I wait
for them to disintegrate, become smooth
black shards like bass notes, my body
an open mouth ready to sing.

Holy Being
    -for Christie

You may have a holy being
on your hands, my Buddhist
minister friend tells me.

            Tell me of my stepson, our mute,
            tube-fed child. Does his skull, heavy
            on the wheelchair headrest, hold
            the language of crisp leaves falling,
            his father's slow-drawn sigh?

She tells me he exists in
the realm of being cared for,
waited on, and loved.

            Tell me did his mother carve
            her name in his bones before
            she died?

She tells me we know
him by the hearts has drawn
to himself in this lifetime.

            Tell me do the tangled branches
            of his brain grow low enough
            for me to climb?

She tells me his appearance serves
as practice, teaching us to come out
of our delusions of what matters.

                                Tell me how to shed my iridescent
         `   carapace, how to bow, and how to fill
                                the empty bowls of my upturned palms?

She tells me he has come so far
in refinement that when entering
this life, his karmic load was light.

                                Tell me about his burdens,
                                do they sound like clanging sirens,
                                or float like broken light from heaven.

She tells me some would say
he is free, reappearing by choice
for others seeking freedom.

                                Tell me he is free.
                                Tell me again.

ABOUT THE AUTHOR

ELLIS ELLIOTT is a facilitator of the online writing group, Bewilderness Writing. She also teaches writing and ballet in an after-school arts education program. Ellis holds an MFA from Queens University. She is a contributing writer for the *Southern Review of Books*, and serves as an editor/workshop instructor for *The Dewdrop* contemplative journal.

Her work can be found in numerous publications including *Signal Mountain Review, Plainsongs Poetry Magazine/Award Poem, Euphony Journal,* and the *Women of Appalachia Project Anthology*. Ellis has a blended family consisting of six grown sons. She resides in Juno Beach, Florida, with her husband, Tim, and a feisty dog named Mabel.